BEYOND

— the —

LOCKER ROOM

BEYOND

—*the*—

LOCKER ROOM

*Emblems of Life Lessons
from Athletics*

PUBLISHED BY

Emblem
MEDIA

AUTHORS
Bret Hall & Brian Oxley

BOOK DESIGN
Erik Peterson

EDITOR
Tim Oxley

ASSOCIATE EDITORS
Lon Lucieer & Greg Bandy

ILLUSTRATOR
Chris Koelle

SPECIAL CONTRIBUTIONS
Rob & Debbie Keith, Jeffrey & Lisa Roy,
Marci Miller, Robert Phillips, Sally Oxley,
Sharon Oxley & Ellen Rehr

With special recognition to the soccer
players of Bridges FC

ISBN   978 1 941012 06 2

Library of Congress Control Number: 2014942769

Published by Emblem Media, LLC
505 Periwinkle, Fort Myers, FL 33908

Find us at: **www.emblemmediallc.com**

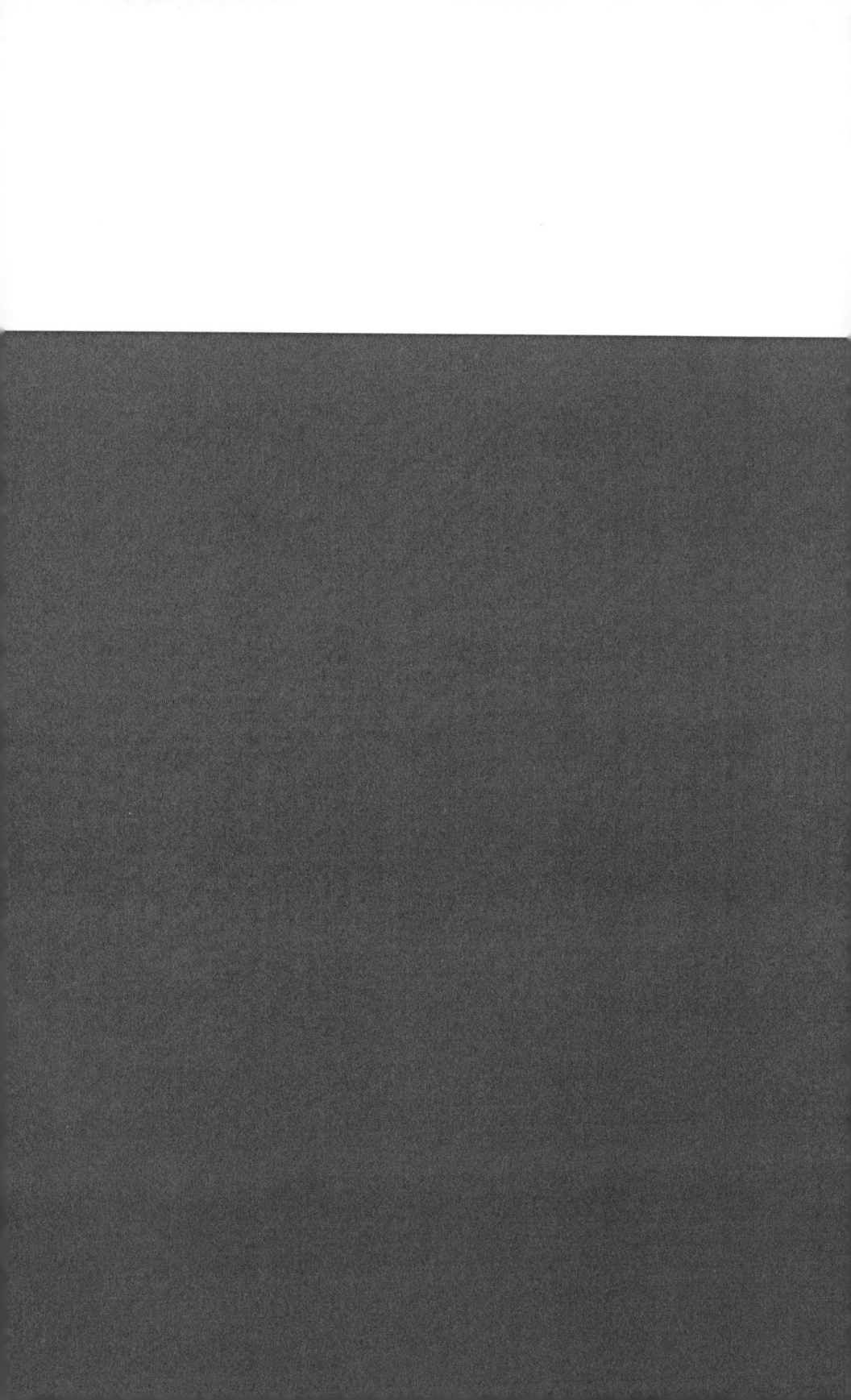

TABLE OF CONTENTS

Bret Hall

From an early age, Bret's life was a challenging one, plagued by difficult circumstances. His poor choices eventually led to multiple stays in and out of a boys' home and other institutions where further troubles surrounded him. Ultimately, it was the authentic love of a strong and gruff Mennonite farmer, John Denlinger, which helped Bret to turn his life around. When Bret was eligible for release from the last institution, he was still a minor, with nowhere to go. John, a counselor at the institution, took a chance on this troubled young heart, agreeing to become his guardian and inviting Bret to come live with him on his farm in Pennsylvania.

Throughout his rebellious years, Bret continued to play soccer and, upon moving in with John, this man became his coach. It soon became apparent that Bret had a real gift for playing soccer, and he excelled at the sport. After playing soccer for one year at a local university, Bret developed a yearning, with John's encouragement, for a faith-based school. He soon transferred to Wheaton College, the same college which Brian had previously attended, although they did not know each other at the time.

While in college, Bret dedicated himself to advancing his skills as a player, and met with considerable success. Never taking this for granted, Bret's continued desire to improve and to gain a competitive edge convinced him to train with the wrestling team at the college in the off-season. His experiences on the wrestling mat under the guidance of the wrestling coach, Pete Wilson, taught him many valuable life lessons.

After college, Bret pursued his goal of becoming a professional soccer player. He did this with both tenacity and passion. Honing his skills he enjoyed a successful professional soccer career spanning 15 years. He had the good fortune to play on multiple championship teams and on several occasions was honored by selection to the all-star team. These events provided Bret not only the opportunity to play with some of the greatest players in the world of his day, but also to continue in the game full-time as a coach after his playing career ended.

Bret has coached at various levels, including a stint as the assistant coach for the U.S. Women's National Team at the World Cup in 2007. His efforts ultimately placed him in his current position as co-founder of Bridges FC, together with Rob Keith, longtime friend and soccer player and a former executive of a large public company. Bridges FC is a non-profit organization established for the purpose of training, equipping, and exposing young, talented soccer players to the demands of professional soccer. The goal of this organization is to develop in its players the physical stamina and mental tenacity necessary to play at a professional level and to witness lives transformed through the power of Jesus Christ.

As a result of a merciful God, Bret was able to overcome the many obstacles encountered during his younger days and eventually succeed as a leader of young men and women in need of guidance and direction. Through Bridges, Bret continues to pour inspiration into the lives of young, talented amateur soccer players who aspire to some day play professionally. In addition to his extensive playing and coaching career in soccer he draws on his considerable life experience to challenge, motivate, and encourage these players. Lessons learned from his misspent youth, days of wrestling practice in college, and his extensive soccer career help to shape and motivate his players to develop mental persistence, discipline, and dedication.

Brian Oxley

During my senior year in high school I discovered a hidden talent—wrestling. I went on to Wheaton College, where I continued to develop this talent. The lessons I learned in the world of sports were a great asset as I entered the world of business. I found there were lessons learned in sports that I could use when dealing with people and life situations.

In recent years, I was introduced by my friend, Rob Keith, to an outstanding soccer coach by the name of Bret Hall. Rob and Bret had been good friends for a number of years, thanks to their mutual interest in soccer. Upon meeting Bret, I was initially struck with the observation that the very coaching methods he used in soccer were, to a great extent, derived from the sport of wrestling. Bret had done some wrestling in college. I found this parallel fascinating. He had incorporated advice gained from some of the greatest wrestling coaches and had applied it to his own sport.

This book represents Bret's coaching philosophy as well as his spiritual insights gained from real life experiences.

INTRODUCTION

Young men and women dream of making their mark on the world, that they might in some way improve it. They may be filled with determination, yet often lack direction while they struggle with self-doubt and low self-esteem. What is it that ultimately provides balance, focus, priority, and inspiration in their lives? Each must make his own choice: *Whom shall I serve?*

In this book, you meet Bret Hall—a former professional soccer player and assistant coach to the U.S. Women's National Team from 2005 to 2007, and co-founder of Bridges FC. He and I, an unorthodox wrestler and businessman, share life lessons we have learned from the arena of athletic competition. Bret and I have many life experiences in common. We both attended Wheaton College. We have each spent a great deal of time on the wrestling mat. Bret has been an effective and influential soccer coach leading young men and women, while as a businessman I have had the opportunity to lead a large number of men and women. During our younger days, each of us encountered difficult challenges and ran into trouble. Studies posed a problem for both of us. Caring people and a benevolent God pulled us back from the darker side of life. Both of us to this day have a passion for seeing young people reach their potential, while finding their purpose in life.

As athletes we share similar backgrounds. The following narratives deal both with failure and success. Bret and I were each motivated to be winners in sports—in my case, wrestling and in Bret's case, soccer. The same must be said for our approach to life in general. Yet what does it really mean to win? What does it take to achieve success? And once you have achieved it, how is it measured?

Today, Bret and I recognize that the most important battles in life are those which are fought on the inside. In this book we have used emblems (or pictures) to tell a story, bringing those invisible battles to life. Our desire is that, by reading this book, young men and women alike might take away lessons that will benefit their daily lives: lessons about winning not only on the field or on the mat, but in life itself—the greatest battle of all.

> Man has always lost his way. He has been a tramp since Eden. For the first time in history he begins really to doubt the object of his wanderings on the earth. He has always lost his way; but now he has lost his address.
> — C.S. Lewis

The authors hope that this book will provide you with enough light to guide you one step at a time in your wanderings as you seek truth in your search to find your ultimate address.

01 WHEN LIFE SLAMS YOU TO THE MAT

In this picture, a wrestler is about to be slammed to the mat as his opponent suddenly lunges, throwing his massive arms around the wrestler's legs. The wrestler about to crash onto the mat watches as the ceiling slides away before his very eyes. Quickly he resorts to the bridge position—an excruciating position—arching his back to form an inverted bridge. Pain screams throughout his entire body as his opponent puts all his weight on him, trying to pin his shoulders to the mat. At this point, accepting defeat would be the easy option, making all the pain go away. He wouldn't have to face another round of brutal punishment. But a strong wrestler knows in the pit of his stomach that although the choice of just giving up might bring temporary relief, this would be at the expense of defeat and deep regret.

This wrestler's predicament is not unlike those trying circumstances we face in life from time to time. The easy way out is to give up, roll over, let the referee slap the mat, and end it all.

Each and every human being can expect to be slammed by life at one time or another; this reflects the human condition. Suddenly, and without warning, pain and suffering can descend upon us. This pain and suffering may come in the form of an accident, an unexpected death of a loved one, rejection by a loved one, an unexpected illness, or the loss of a job. Trials and tribulations and the pain and suffering they bring are no respecters of people.

When tragedy strikes, however, what makes the difference is how we respond. Some are stunned and tend to ask, "Why me?" These are the ones who fail to get up from the ground, letting the tragedy defeat them. They fall victim to self-pity.

Others respond to tragedy by getting up and moving forward. They recognize that there is no time to wallow in self-pity. In the words of Helen Keller, who overcame the adversities of being blind and deaf to become one of the leading humanitarians of the 20th century, *Self-pity is our worst enemy and if we yield to it, we can never do anything wise in this world.* So, we cannot pout or feel sorry for ourselves, even when we might have good reason for this. It is all about the attitude.

We must be prepared for what life throws at us. What does it take to knock the fight out of you? And in soccer, what if your goalie gives up an easy goal to the opposing team? What will happen to this man's self-esteem? What is he really made of? Suppose a forward misses an easy shot? The game must go on. We can't continue to spend our lives regretting past failures if we expect to deal with day-to-day realities.

02 NO RETREAT

Has life ever become so difficult that your mind is continually preoccupied with the idea of escape? In this picture, two wrestlers are battling it out on the mat. Their whole world has shrunk down to just the two of them within the circle of competition. For the wrestler, this circle is the mat; for the businessman, it's the market; for a soccer player, it's the field. If you walk away, you will lose. It's that simple.

When the whistle blows and the game begins, will you be prepared to face the challenges before you? Some pull back from the difficulties and challenges, choosing to sit in the stands with the spectators. Some are defeated before the game even begins. They are defeated in their mind, for they have convinced themselves that they cannot win—that their opponent is too strong. They attribute imaginary qualities and strength to their opponents or obstacles. Some take the cautious approach by pulling back, circling around the edge of the challenge, and are penalized for not engaging their opponent.

If we're going to win the battle of life, we have to stay engaged; retreat is not an option. To hang in there requires hard work. Having the physical stamina and the mental determination to endure hard work is a gift. And don't sell practice short. If during practice sessions you fail to apply yourself...that is, if you don't pull your weight during soccer practice, you'll most likely perform poorly during the game. You will lose your competitive edge. It all boils down to attitude.

To paraphrase Dan Gable, the famous wrestling coach, on the subject of winning at wrestling:

> *In the first period, it's the wrestler with the better technique that wins. In the second, it's the man with more endurance. And in the third, it's the guy with the most heart.*

03 STANDING FIRM

While growing up, most of us lack real courage. Sometimes circumstances arise which require a measure of courage, but in the long run we would prefer to avoid such troubles. We would all like to be brave, but it is the same as anything else, you have to prepare yourself mentally and physically for such bravery.

It takes courage to form a wall in soccer, without the use of your hands for protection, while a kicker sends a ball rocketing toward you in an effort to score a goal. It is not natural to resist the temptation to duck, but with discipline and training, natural instincts can be overcome. What was just said about soccer practice holds true here: If you duck during practice, you'll probably duck during the game.

Obstacles or challenges in our path are like weights in a weight room. With each repetition and increase in the resistance level, an athlete builds strength and stamina. So too in life, each obstacle or challenge we overcome strengthens us and gives us courage to face the next one. This added measure of courage can ultimately lead to acts of bravery. As with virtually everything of value and worth, developing bravery requires perseverance and sacrifice.

One such example can be found in a story from the Old Testament in the Bible. Most of us have heard the story of young David slaying the giant, Goliath, with a single stone thrown from his sling. However, David's courage to stand up to Goliath, this warrior chosen by Israel's enemies, was not developed at the moment he first faced Goliath. It was refined in the fiery furnace of life. David was the youngest of eight brothers and would have had to learn how to stand up to teasing and roughhousing with his seven older brothers in order to survive. In addition, as a shepherd, we are told that while herding his father's sheep in the wilderness, David often had to protect them from lions and bears, slaying these in the process. Experiencing God's deliverance and protection through these harrowing experiences developed David's courage to the point where he was capable of defying and defeating this Goliath.

Standing firm with courage in the face of adversity is a skill we all need to develop. This skill, however, needs to be carefully honed, for it is only when we are victorious in the lesser battles that we will be brave enough to overcome the greater obstacles and challenges we face.

04 THE ROOT OF COURAGE

Swamps are foreboding places. You never know how deep the water is or what might be lurking beneath all that green and brown scum. So what gives somebody the courage to enter a "swamp" to help some suffering human being? What would possess an athlete to leave the confines of his conventional life, to walk into a swamp where ugly things lurk? But if we truly believe this man mired in the muck of life has real worth and dignity, then we ought to be prepared to jump in and help out, right? In sports, there is a common expression among teammates, "I've got your back." When things get down and dirty in the heat of the contest, when tempers flare and exhaustion sets in, it is reassuring to know that you have teammates standing behind you.

But from where does courage come to go in harm's way? Where do you get that brave madness? Courage comes from something deep within the human heart, something called...love. The greatest love story ever told isn't about a romantic relationship between a man and a woman. The story is actually about the purest, most perfectly powerful God, who humbly entered the immense swamp of humanity in which every vile deed wallows. And He came to save all of us. It's a love story that should overwhelm every one of us—and serve as an example for all to follow. We should never forget how God has met His children in the darkest, slimiest places of their souls, and has brought them into the light.

People lost in a swamp may or may not show up at our doorsteps, but we should always be looking for those stuck in the muck of life—those who are hurting—and lift them up. Do we have that kind of love which is willing to enter the swamp? Our culture is full of lost, wounded, widowed, and orphaned souls. How are we reaching out to them?

05 NOBODY LIKES TO LOSE

Nobody likes to lose. Whatever the sport, we all want to win; but are we willing to put in the hard work and sacrifice to make that happen? At some point all athletes face this dilemma. Is the pain and sacrifice worth it? Will you fold up your tent and walk away? When you hit the wall, are you able to summon the strength and will to push through? Those who manage this can achieve great things.

While losing is never enjoyable, sometimes you have to be willing to face defeat and humiliation in order to succeed. In wrestling, being pinned with your back to the mat is the most humiliating way to suffer a loss. Some are unable to deal with such embarrassment, choosing instead to simply quit the sport. In the words of John F. Kennedy, the 35th president of the United States, *Victory has a thousand fathers, but defeat is an orphan*. However, those who really wish to excel will learn from a devastating loss and use this defeat as motivation for improvement. They will seek another opportunity to do better the next time around.

So, when life throws us for a loss, how will we react? Will we give in to depression and defeat or will we treat this as a learning experience, teaching us to grow and achieve greater things?

06 GET OUT OF THE LOCKER ROOM!

Preparation and training are vital for success in any endeavor. However, there comes a point when preparation and training must ultimately come to an end. Eventually, we must leave the relative safety and comfort of the locker room and storm the field. Otherwise, the game of life will pass us by. Only when the game plan is put into play will we be able to determine its effect. Our teammates are counting on us. John Stuart Mill, the most influential British philosopher of the 19th century, put it this way: *A man who has nothing for which he is willing to fight, nothing which is more important than his own personal safety, is a miserable creature and has no chance of being free unless made and kept so by the exertions of better men than himself.*

What is holding us back—a lack of self-confidence, fear of failure, fear of disappointing someone, fear of success and the responsibility that may come with it, or some other unknown fear? Now is the time to act! Not later, not tomorrow, but right now! Not "when I get around to it." That, in plain English, means never. Unless we are prepared to take action, we run the risk of making the locker room our permanent home. We must get out of the locker room!

07 THE PRICE OF VICTORY: GETTING YOUR HANDS DIRTY

Victory rarely appears from out of nowhere, like some knight in shining armor mounted on a great white steed. And it's not like charging up a hill on horseback; it's more like crawling up that hill on your belly. Often the price of victory requires humility; humility in the form of a man, muddy and bruised. Instead of seeing a picture of polished performance, we are confronted with the unsettling image of an athlete astride a warthog, dashing through some nasty sewer. Yet, this athlete perseveres. He overcomes the obstacles placed in his path. Once pride has stepped aside in your life, you can get on with the business of achieving victory.

Theodore Roosevelt, the 26th president of the United States, put it this way:

> It is not the critic who counts; not the man who points out how the strong man stumbles or where the doer of deeds could have done them better. The credit belongs to the man who is actually in the arena, whose face is marred by dust and sweat and blood...

He spoke of those *timid souls who know neither victory nor defeat.*

Whether challenges come to us on the soccer field, or meet us in everyday life, if we are to overcome them it will require dedication and commitment. The more demanding the challenge, the greater the effort needed to overcome it. Making this effort, in turn, should bring out the best in us. But be advised: There are no shortcuts. Some challenges are so imposing that they demand more than we are prepared to offer. Sometimes we simply have to accept the pain that comes with the training process in order to reap the benefit—the ultimate reward. Don't shy away from the pain; never give up!

08 PUTTING YOUR WHOLE HEART INTO IT

We have all dreamed of hitting the winning shot as the buzzer sounds, like LeBron James, or scoring the decisive goal like the great David Beckham. But until we change such dreams into achievable goals, that is all they are—idle dreams. Without the hard work necessary to change these dreams into realistic goals, they will remain nothing more than illusions. It is only after hours of practice, day after day, when you have nothing left to offer—no courage, no heart, no confidence, no talent, and nothing but a remnant of strength and your iron will—that your dream begins its transformation into reality.

Whenever LeBron James made that winning basket or David Beckham that decisive goal, the crowd would erupt in cheers, aware only of this immediate victory. In reality, however, these victories were actually won in some dusty gym in the middle of the night, or in some obscure field in the middle of nowhere, when no one was there to watch. Practice, practice, practice...refining and honing skills until exhaustion sets in and a battle of wills takes place—the will to ease up and rest, pitted against the will to excel and achieve greatness. It is often the ability to overcome the former by the latter that separates one athlete from another.

It is the heart, the human spirit within us, which will ultimately determine the outcome of this battle. From our heart comes our greatest strength, so whatever we do, we must put our whole heart into it!

09 DISCIPLINING THE UNRULY MIND

An unruly mind may behave much like a wild horse, untamed it runs where it will. The mind wanders from one pleasure to another or to some realm of fantasy. Disciplining the unruly mind is like taming a wild mustang—it is not an easy thing to do. Just as you need to cut out a mustang from the rest of the herd in order to build trust, so too the mind must be free from needless distractions, so that it can concentrate on the matter at hand. Concentration and the control of our thoughts are the keys to making sure the mind does not drift, becoming an impediment to success. In much the same way the mind is trained and disciplined, so too is the body.

To be successful in life, just as in sports, the mind must be disciplined and focused on a single purpose. There is only one priority, not a handful of options. As the famous basketball player Bill Russell once said, *Concentration and mental toughness are the margins of victory.*

10 TALENT ONLY TAKES YOU SO FAR

The relationship between talent and hard work is not always clear. We all know of the athlete who is blessed with an extraordinary talent...a talent which comes to him naturally; we might call him "a natural." But we are also familiar with another type of athlete— perhaps the "most improved player" who has built his reputation through "intestinal fortitude", that is, "guts" and hard work. The following quotation from the famous sports movie "Rudy" about an unlikely Notre Dame football player comes to mind: *You're five foot nothin'. A hundred and nothin'. And you have barely a speck of athletic ability. And you hung in there with the best college football players in the land for two years.... In this life, you don't have to prove nothin' to nobody but yourself. Am I making myself clear?*

Yes, some players lead an undisciplined life, living off the dream that their talent will carry them through without the concerted effort and discipline of training. But, in the long run, talent will get you only so far. Without the hard work and discipline of training, eventually your competition will overtake you. Relying solely on your talent is like sitting on the bench, feeding your gut and your ego, while others play their heart out.

The higher the level of competition, the greater the commitment required to excel. You must be prepared to compete every single minute of every single game. You do not have the luxury of taking a play off here and there. In the words of Kevin Durant, an all-star basketball player for the Oklahoma City Thunder, in the movie "Thunderstruck", *Hard work beats talent when talent fails to work hard.*

So, too, in life, the greater the task before us, the more preparation, planning, and effort are required to accomplish it. Our competition is just around the corner. We can't always rely on what worked in the past. Reputation will only get us so far. We have to be looking forward to innovation and improvement.

11 | THE DREAM FORGED IN THE VALLEY

Whether it is a wrestler winning a gold medal at the Olympics or a soccer player winning the World Cup, we all desire to reach the pinnacle of success. However, such dreams become reality—not on the mountaintop, but in the valley. Victory can easily be seen high upon the mountain; but in the valley things are not so clear. At times we are lost. We cannot always see our ultimate goal, but we keep moving forward. We often spend most of our life in the valley, which can be frightening and lonely at times, but it is this struggle in the dark valley that urges us forward to climb the mountain that rises before us.

In the valley, as the athlete faces severe tests and challenges, he builds the strength to persevere, to reach new heights. In the words of Arnold Schwarzenegger, renowned bodybuilder and former governor of California, *Strength does not come from winning. Your struggles develop your strengths. When you go through hardships and decide not to surrender, that is strength.* The very darkness in the valley will train you to see more clearly the opportunities before you. The apostle Paul makes a similar point in II Corinthians 4:8-9 when speaking about the dark valleys of persecution he was encountering: *We are hard pressed on every side, but not crushed; perplexed, but not in despair; persecuted, but not abandoned; struck down, but not destroyed.*

12 WHAT IS A FRIEND?

The torch represents the light of this athlete's life. He is trying to keep his torch aloft, but the rough, turbulent waters washing against him are obstructing his progress, causing him to stumble. In sports, you quickly learn that you cannot win on your own; you need to depend on your teammates. When facing the adversity of a strong opposing team, the heroic efforts of one individual are never enough to bring victory. Michael Jordan learned this early in his basketball career. It was not until he submitted to the leadership of Phil Jackson, his coach, and consciously made an effort to work within the team game plan with his teammates Scottie Pippen and Horace Grant, that he won his first championship.

So, too, in life, when the sea gets rough and we are faced with trials and tribulations, we all need to rely on our friends for support. Marcus Tullius Cicero, an orator and statesman of Ancient Rome and considered the greatest Latin prose stylist, once said, *The shifts of fortune test the reliability of friends.* What a precious gift these friends are who help steady us and share our joys and problems. These are trusted friends who lend their support and strength to lift us up; friends who have listened to our needs and kept our conversations confidential. Friends like this are necessary if we are to live our lives in the light.

13 PREPARED FOR ANY CHALLENGE

Training and preparation are keys to success in any sport. The proper equipment is also a critical component in any athletic contest. For example, a soccer player would never dream of stepping out onto the field without shin guards in place, or the wrestler onto the mat without head gear, for obvious reasons. These are visible forms of protection, which everyone can see. However, the trained athlete also takes with him onto the field or mat certain invisible forms of protection that are not so obvious. Each athlete who is prepared to compete has also trained and disciplined his body to withstand the physical challenges and the inevitable contact that he will experience in the course of competition.

Just as the body and mind must be trained to excel in any sport, so, too, must the spirit be strengthened to withstand the challenges of evil. The battles we face in life are not played out in a sports arena, but are actually spiritual battles between good and evil; battles which continually take place in the world around us. Fortunately, there are certain protections available to us here as well. The Bible tells us to *Put on the whole armor of God....* This preparation will directly affect our ability to prevail in any spiritual battle.

14 TAKING A STAND FOR JUSTICE

Every sport is governed by a set of rules. These rules are designed to ensure fair play. As players, we are required to understand these rules and to play within the limits set by them. Those who fail to play by the rules quickly develop reputations as dirty players. Further, unless we play by these rules, violations and penalties will be the result.

In life, the rules are not always so obvious and clear-cut. While we all advocate concepts of fairness and justice, it is often not easy to determine the fair and just course in every situation. However, at other times, when we meet injustice head on, there is no denying its existence.

So what should we do when we confront a clear case of injustice? Cower in our homes? Wash our hands of the issue? Look the other way? Fighting injustice is everyone's business. Seek out injustice and take a stand for justice. Here, the words of the great civil rights leader of the 20th century, Martin Luther King, seem appropriate, *Human progress is neither automatic nor inevitable... Every step toward the goal of justice requires sacrifice, suffering, and struggle; the tireless exertions and passionate concern of dedicated individuals.* He goes on to assert, *Injustice anywhere is a threat to justice everywhere.*

While seeking to correct injustice done to others, we must also learn how to deal with injustice against us. When we find ourselves the victims of injustice, we must not yield to sentiments of anger and resentment at our own misfortune. Rather, with calm persuasion we must pursue our just cause. In the process, we must never cease to be just and gracious when dealing with others.

15 GOD'S HELPING HAND

The following words taken from an old picture book called *Choice Emblems* (1772) are here paraphrased: *The moth, tempted by the brightness of the candle flame, circles around it, until at last it is caught in the flame and consumed.* Similarly, people who often know the right path make only a half-hearted attempt to resist those enticements which lead them astray. The misguided pursuit of money, status, self-promotion—even affection—without self-control can lead to self-destruction. This holds true particularly for the successful athlete. Such temptations and enticements are sure to follow close on the heels of success. Those who lack discernment and wisdom will get burned.

G.K. Chesterton, a great British writer and philosopher of the late 19th and early 20th century and known as the "prince of paradox", once said, *Tragedy is the point where things are left to God and men can do no more.* After getting burned, the turning point of your life may well be the act of turning to God, the One who promises to restore and uplift those who call out to Him.

16 GROUNDED IN HUMILITY

A sumo wrestler attempts to force another wrestler to step out of the ring or to touch the ground with any part of his body other than the soles of his feet. With skill and leverage, a smaller, more nimble wrestler can topple a far larger opponent. A wrestler who is grounded and determined can move large obstacles.

Similarly, a person who is grounded in humility can uplift those in trouble and distress, and help them overcome their problems. If success comes your way, maintain an attitude of humility and you will be able to bless others. In the words of St. Augustine, one of the most influential Christian philosophers and theologians of Western civilization, *The sufficiency of my merit is to know that my merit is not sufficient.* In other words, to paraphrase: Our accomplishments are never enough to bring satisfaction and fulfillment in and of themselves. It is only as we reach out to help others in humility that our humanity is fully realized.

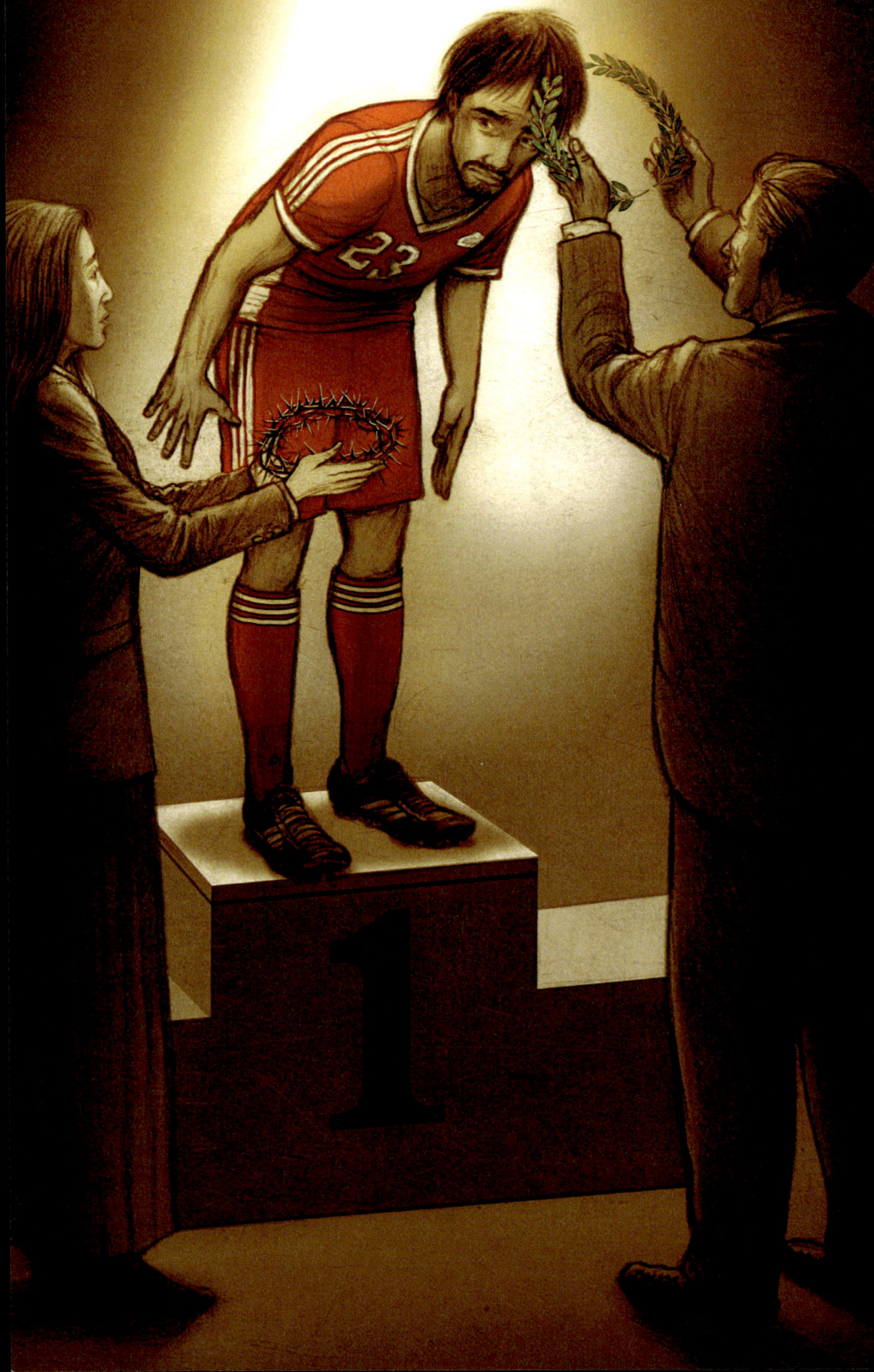

17 WEAR GREATNESS LIGHTLY

Greatness comes with its "close companion, a crown of thorns" (*Choice Emblems*). The laurel wreath of victory invites a crown of responsibility. Those who are elevated to a position of honor are, whether they accept this responsibility or not, faced with the fact that they are now viewed as a role model. It is often too easy to accept the public accolades, and then conveniently forget our debt to this same public. Those who fail to live up to this high calling, who act irresponsibly by leading a careless life, set a bad example for others. On the other hand, those who accept this responsibility can make a good impression on many people, especially on young people. We must choose which path we will follow.

In addition, lurking near the spoils of victory is the great enemy of all who achieve success: Pride. We have all faced its allure. Be prepared for the battle to overcome pride. Once pride has us in its grip, we begin to lose sight of all the help and the support that we received from family, friends, teammates, and mentors along the way. We want to take all the credit. This pride is an affront to God, for everything we have—our talents, our strengths, and our minds—comes from Him. As the well-known Swiss psychologist Carl Jung put it, *Through pride, we are ever deceiving ourselves. But deep down below the surface of the average conscience a still, small voice says to us, something is out of tune.* We must learn to listen to that still, small voice.

Purging ourselves of pride is not an easy matter. Are we obsessed with the rewards that come with success? Do we use them to promote our own self-image or do we want to inspire others to achieve great things? As J.C. Macaulay, a Christian theologian and writer, once put it, *One of the marks of true greatness is the ability to develop greatness in others.*

18. GIVING BACK

A crowd surrounds this soccer star, clamoring for his autograph and for his attention. Hidden in a dark corner stands this shy little girl, too bashful to reach out to her hero. Frequently, those who are lonely and in pain remain isolated—cut off from others or simply hidden in the shadows; these unfortunate victims might never approach anyone for help.

Those among us who have been blessed in so many ways have a responsibility to "give back" to those less fortunate than ourselves; whether they be the poor, the social rejects, the oppressed, or the hurting. Jeanette Winterson, an acclaimed British author, put it bluntly, *It's true that heroes are inspiring, but mustn't they also do some rescuing if they are to be worthy of their name? Would Wonder Woman matter if she only sent commiserating telegrams to the distressed?* Caring people need to seek out those in distress and lift them up. Never forget how God has met His children in the dark places of their souls, and has brought them into the light. As the Psalmist has said, *The Lord lifts up those who are bowed down...* (Psalms 146:8b).

19 COURAGE TO FACE OUR FEARS

We are all subject to fears of one kind or another—fear of heights, fear of the dark, fear of loneliness, fear of confined spaces, fear of public speaking, and so on. Perhaps in your childhood you were afraid of thunder and lightning and recall running to your parents' room for protection and comfort. However, greater fears than these exist; fears that derive from the evil which exists within man's heart. We live in a fallen world and man is a fallen creature. As a result, man is capable of committing unspeakable acts against his fellow man. History is replete with examples of man's cruelty to other men, such as Hitler's tyranny and that of Mao Zedong.

Athletes, too, face fears, which are every bit as real. What is the nature of these fears and who are the people we fear the most?

The wrestler we must face for the championship match...
The coach who might dismiss us from the team...
The mocking crowd who ridicules us for missing a crucial goal...
The parent whose approval we desperately long for...

Whatever the source of the fear, it takes courage to face our fears. In order to summon such courage, it is helpful to keep in mind that Death, personified as the Grim Reaper, is the great equalizer here.

We all have a rendezvous with that six-foot hole in the ground. We must each deal with this eventuality—at a time and place not of our choosing. Sooner or later, even the most powerful and feared leader, boss, or mocker—each and everyone—is carried off to his eternal destiny by a fate beyond his control.

In light of all this, the question remains: Why do we fear these mortals who will be carried off like the rest of us at their appointed time, when we should fear the One who makes the ultimate decision? He is the *only* being, an omnipotent being, who can determine our eternal destiny. He sends His angels to carry us through that Valley of Death. When the question of our eternal destiny is settled, we can experience true peace; just as this aged soccer player, whose playing years have long since passed, is being carried away in His loving arms.

20 THE QUIET PLACE

Within the arena there is an ambience of light, noise, and excitement. The crowd is fired up with eager anticipation for the game to commence. A surge of adrenalin brings the athletes to the point of readiness for this demanding competition. This helps them concentrate on the game. The action is about to begin.

Standing atop this arena, above all the noise and commotion, we meet a lone athlete as she seeks a moment of inspiration. This is her place of refuge; she has come here tonight, just as she has done prior to each game. Gazing up into the night sky, she gains the proper perspective. The glory to be won tonight on the field below pales in comparison to the vast glory of the heavens. The victory, which comes through human endeavor—through physical strength—is certainly fleeting. But the creative power of God endures forever.

In the Bible, the prophet Isaiah expressed the sentiment of this athlete when he said, *Lift up your eyes to the heavens, and look at the earth beneath; ...my salvation will be forever, and my righteousness will never be dismayed.* (Isaiah 51:6)

The athlete will carry this perspective with her as she returns to the arena, once more aware of God's majesty and of man's insignificance. George MacDonald, a 19th century Scottish author, poet, and Christian minister, once said, *If we will but let our God and Father work His will with us, there can be no limit to His enlargement of our existence.* Have you stepped away from the lights and noise of your arena—to a quiet place? It might just give you the perspective you need.

THE SOURCE
OF TRUE STRENGTH

While physical strength can be a great asset in athletics, the strength we rely on to achieve our goals is internal and comes from the mind and the heart. But what happens when this strength fails us? Where do we turn? The pressures in life can sometimes be more than the human body and mind can handle. In these circumstances, there is another source of strength, which is available to us from Heaven. We can either simply give up or turn to that true source of unlimited strength, God.

God, who cares for us, invites us to cast all of our burdens upon Him. God promises that, *[His] grace is sufficient for you, for [His] power is made perfect in weakness…* (II Corinthians 12:9). When we reach the limit of our resources—we need to look up, and reach up! The God of light in Heaven is reaching down to us in love, waiting for a simple response of faith in Him. Accept His invitation! Then watch what He will do in us and through us.

We close with a poem from George Herbert, a 17th century poet, which speaks about this source of light. May we all find joy and fulfillment as we seek this light.

Teach me Thy love to know;
That this new light, which now I see,
May both the work and workman show;
Then by a sunbeam I will climb to Thee.

Word of mouth is crucial for any author to succeed. If you enjoyed the book, please consider leaving a review where you purchased it, or on *Goodreads,* even if it's only a line or two; it would make all the difference and would be very much appreciated. You can also follow us on Twitter or "like" our page on Facebook. Thank you.

SAY HELLO!

WEBSITE	www.emblemmediallc.com
TWITTER	@EmblemMediaLLC
FACEBOOK	www.facebook.com/emblemmediallc
EMAIL	info@emblemmediallc.com

MORE FROM EMBLEM MEDIA

THE HOUND OF HEAVEN—A MODERN ADAPTATION
by Brian and Sally Oxley & Sonja Peterson with Dr. Devin Brown

Francis Thompson's classic, *The Hound of Heaven,* is considered by many to be a poetic masterpiece. The autobiographical poem has touched lives for years and is without doubt one of the finest pieces of Christian verse ever written. This one-of-a-kind book has both the original poem, as well as a modern adaptation. Each version has a unique set of illustrations to enhance the reader's experience. Emblem Media has also produced an animated video version of the modern adaptation, which can be viewed at emblemmediallc.com. The song at the end of the video, entitled *I Finally See,* was also inspired by the poem. It is available for purchase on iTunes along with a collection of songs written and produced for Emblem Media on the CD project *An Amazing Story.*

To stay in touch with Emblem Media for updates on *The Hound of Heaven* materials and other Emblem Media releases, please "like" us on Facebook.

WEBSITE   www.emblemmediallc.com
FACEBOOK   www.facebook.com/thehoundofheaven

AVAILABLE ON KINDLE EBOOK AND IN PAPERBACK.

INTOLERANCE
by Brian Oxley

Experienced governments can turn an international crisis to their advantage, especially if they seek to maintain domestic order. Imagine a world crisis, one which confounds even the best of the world's politicians and economists. Is the solution to this crisis worth sacrificing hard-won freedoms? What sort of a regime would wish to play the devil in order to impose compliance and conformity? What regime could possibly stress the need for order and stability over the need for personal freedom? It is a regime which proclaims "tolerance" to be the ultimate good for society.

Enter Hiram Levy, a resolute, insightful man. A former U.S. Serviceman, Hiram has the courage to stand up to the new regime. Witness his transformation, as his "run-ins" with this new political regime harden his resolve to resist. He is vilified as an intolerant man in a world where tolerance is the only virtue. He stands face-to-face with another strong man—Captain Shih—as they face down a lie.

AVAILABLE IN PAPERBACK.

THE LAST TOWER
by Brian Oxley

Imagine a sinister threat is looming, whose potential for malice is barely discernible...for now.

A series of destructive waves—shocks to the world system—takes place during the first two decades of the new millennium that initially appears to have no connection. But the ensuing shock waves do not pass and fade. They grow and converge to undermine our confidence in the entire world order.

Five friends begin to creatively imagine the results of a world dominated by a leadership with a hidden agenda. Peppering the conversation with stories that illustrate their hopes and fears, they engage in a charged dialogue. Hearts and minds confront one another to find glimmers of Truth and the unsettling possibility of supernatural involvement.

More than a prophetic fable, it's a call for some soul-searching introspection. And hey, it's just five regular guys at the Star Diner engaged in a little...spirited discussion. We're just talking...

AVAILABLE ON KINDLE EBOOK AND IN PAPERBACK.

BRIAN'S CORNER NEWSLETTER
by Brian Oxley

At the dawn of the printing press, a special kind of book rose to the top of the best-seller lists that featured a unique blend of images and text. These picture-text publications were known as Emblem books. Today, when we use the word *emblem,* we typically think of an image or object that stands for something else.

Brian Oxley's passion has always been to encourage and inspire people to a higher level of workmanship. Drawing from life experiences as a son growing up in Japan, a husband, father, and executive of a large, multinational company, he offers "food for thought" on issues regarding leadership, teamwork, and values in everyday life and business.

Through *Brian's Corner,* he shares *short* essays and stories illustrated with dramatic, original artwork...in essence, "an Emblem email." Consider this an invitation to invest a few minutes each month to reflect on some important topics in the days ahead. Please visit our website to learn more and sign up!

WEBSITE   www.brians-corner.com
TWITTER   @brianscorner

OTHER BOOKS
BY BRIAN OXLEY

EMBLEMS OF LEADERSHIP IMAGINED—
SILENT PARABLES *(Revised & Expanded)*
by Brian Oxley

This second edition of *Emblems of Leadership Imagined—Silent Parables* has been revised and expanded with seven new Emblems and eight revised Emblems along with updated content.

Using original art that conceptualizes the thoughts that are stimulated by the accompanying commentary, Brian Oxley draws the reader on a soul-searching journey for the meaning of leadership imagined. As he explains in his introduction, "We may sometimes forget that leadership is a privilege more than an entitlement. It has its rewards and acclaim, but also, at times, its heavy burdens— being accountable to customers, employees, shareholders, and our families. We need strength from the moral and spiritual realm that is greater than ourselves." Brian challenges the reader to join him in meditating on developing the effective skills needed to make an impact on the people we lead.

AVAILABLE IN PAPERBACK.

COMING SOON
FROM EMBLEM MEDIA

LILIAS TROTTER
Documentary & Book (coming 2015)

You may have never heard of Lilias Trotter, but after seeing and reading her story, you will never forget her. Blessed with the privileged life of British aristocracy and artistic talent beyond compare, she left it all to do mission work in hostile Algeria as a single woman in the late 1800s. The beautiful journals she left behind from these difficult and dangerous years are filled with faithful insight and spectacular artwork.

We are currently in preproduction to bring this amazing woman's testimony and diaries to life through a documentary film and an artistically accurate re-creation of her journals.

THE REFLECTING POOL
by Brian Oxley

It is said that in the moment just before your death, your entire life flashes before your eyes in an instant. In *The Reflecting Pool*, a shrewd businessman, distracted by his anger over corporate frustrations, crashes his car and now lies in a hospital bed in a deep coma hovering between life and death. His past unfolds before him in a strange dream in which his deceased father leads him back to the deep pool where, in his childhood, they would fish and talk about life. There on its crystalline surface he sees the events of his life reflected with compelling clarity, encouraging him to pursue a better future, that is, if he survives.

Made in the USA
San Bernardino, CA
12 November 2014